The Last Exile

poems by

Gustavo Pérez Firmat

Finishing Line Press
Georgetown, Kentucky

The Last Exile

Copyright © 2016 by Gustavo Pérez Firmat
ISBN 978-1-944251-71-0 First Edition
All rights reserved under International and Pan-American Copyright Conventions. No part of this book may be reproduced in any manner whatsoever without written permission from the publisher, except in the case of brief quotations embodied in critical articles and reviews.

ACKNOWLEDGMENTS

Grateful acknowledgment is made to the magazines in which these poems first appeared:

Cold Mountain Review: "Legacies," "Old Octopus"
County Lines: "Land for Sale," "Inside Andy Taylor"
Gravel: "Dirty Old Man Loses His Place"
New Southerner: "Land for Sale"
Off the Coast: "Dirty Old Man Takes a Nap"
Review: Literature and Arts of the Americas: "Chivas," "Fatherly Thoughts on Mother's Day," "Nochebuena"

Editor: Christen Kincaid

Cover Art: Nathan Wirth

Author Photo: Many Anne Pérez

Cover Design: Elizabeth Maines

Printed in the USA on acid-free paper.
Order online: www.finishinglinepress.com
　　　　　　also available on amazon.com

Author inquiries and mail orders:
Finishing Line Press
P. O. Box 1626
Georgetown, Kentucky 40324
U. S. A.

Table of Contents

I.

Land for Sale 1
Lilac Land 2
Nochebuena 3
Chivas 4
Legacies 5
The Island 7
Fatherly Thoughts on Mother's Day 8
Piedra 9
The Last Exile 10
Inside Andy Taylor 11
Old Octopus 12
After Exile 13

II.

Dirty Old Man Watches the Birds 16
Dirty Old Man Looks for Same 18
Dirty Old Man Regrets 19
Dirty Old Man Applies for Medicare 20
Dirty Old Man Feeling Bereft 21
Dirty Old Man Takes a Nap 22
Dirty Old Man Loses His Place 23
Dirty Old Man Foams at the Mouth 24
Dirty Old Man Thinks about the Future 25
Dirty Old Man Eschews a Fling 26
Dirty Old Man Talks to Himself in the Dark 27
Dirty Old Man Talks to His Neighbors 28
Dirty Old Man Argues with His Wife 29
Dirty Old Man Endeavors To Be Optimistic 30

For David

I.

Land for Sale

Someone was born here. Someone died.
The night they moved in, they made love
so hard, she worried the neighbors would
hear them. Afterwards she closed the blinds.

They were two at first, then three, then four,
then three again and two once more. Life.
One afternoon a tornado came through—
purple light, wind whooshing, doors rattling.

They huddled in the bathroom. The dish
blew off the roof. Twigs flew. Nothing
happened. Life. Once he kicked a wall in.
Once she hid a wedding dress. Nothing

pleased them more than weekend nights
by themselves. They feasted. Never travelled,
they didn't want the house to miss them.
(So he said. The truth is he was afraid.)

CDs, books and photos lived on the shelves.
The new sofa and chair were fifteen years old.
When he wasn't alone, he was with her.
What one forgot, the other remembered.

Children came to visit. They were fed.
The woods in back matured. Robins returned.
One day he woke up early, turned to her
and said, Good morning, babe. She wasn't there.

Lilac Land

Near the street where he lives,
the scent of otherwise.
Of parents who aren't orphans

of children who aren't parents.
No lies or lack in lilac land.
He strolls in and out, heart aching.

A violet-water man lost among lilacs
with only her hand to hold him.
Violet water, violent water, wave

and burden, churning, churning,
the lathe in the wave, the wave
in the bones of a lazy island,

no sooner glimpsed than unminded,
its alligator carcass washing up
still, still on the lap of lilac land.

Nochebuena

You need to know, first of all, that mirrors
grow fond of the faces that look into them.
Then you need to know about the exception:
motel mirrors, made ruthless by the stares of strangers.

Now think of Nochebuena, and think of mirrors.
Time was when Nochebuena gazed back at you
lovingly. Oh, you were handsome then, and full
of harmless fun and uncles and drink and dancing.

But that's not who you were, that was Nochebuena
touching up your reflection. You weren't so different
from what you are now, except there were more of you.
Tomorrow night, if you happen to look at yourself

in the mirror and the face that glares back is unfamiliar,
a hurricane survivor's face, don't blame the mirror.
Blame the other faces, the careless faces that look
into Nochebuena and see themselves at Motel Six.

Chivas

My father brought home a bottle of Chivas
that swung on a metal hammock.
For years he kept refilling it
with cheap scotch. Sundays came and went.
Birthdays, Thanksgivings, Nochebuenas.
No one seemed to notice. I was that bottle.

Two decades later I buy a gallon bottle
of rot-gut, empty it into the kitchen sink,
fill it with Chivas. People come and go
talking of *fricandó*, people come and go
talking of Fidel Castro. And no one says anything
even though, with time, I've become that bottle too.

What am I to think? That my friends can't tell
good scotch from bad, or that I haven't aged well?

Legacies

1.
The one thing you have from your father,
you didn't get from your father.
You stole it from your son,
who inherited it from his grandfather.
A gold ring, oval aquamarine framed
by tiny diamonds. He flaunted it,
Cuban to the end, until your mother took it off his finger.
Hurricanes, *nortes*, sweater weather, *canícula*
registered on its watery face: gray, blue, bluer, bluest.

2.
The Antiques Road Show: in Mobile,
a Civil War sword and scabbard that belonged
to someone's greatgrandfather; in Pittsburgh,
the fake 18th century writing desk, a family heirloom;
in Chicago, the Remington lithograph; in St. Louis,
the Navajo quilt; in Chapel Hill, a purloined ring.

3.
It's an advantage not to get by on yourself.
To be able to brag (to no one but yourself):
I am that man's grandson, that man
was my father, and that other man, my son.
It makes you alone more than you alone.

4.
Look back and you see an island,
sand and stucco and a Spaniard named
José, just off the boat and already balding,
pedaling a bike, peddling potatoes in Old Havana.
Look back again and you see an island,
a clump of hibiscus and a park bench
where another Spaniard, his name was Pedro,
railed against sugar, praised the potato.

5.

Say to yourself: A man rich
in hand-me-downs is a rich man.

6.

Yet there are days, weekday afternoons
late in summer, when the longer you look,
the less you feel for José's island,
and Pedro's too, the less it touches you.
Then you put on the Tony Bennett CD
and say: this is the tongue I use for feeling.

7.

The family comes over, Sunday lunch,
and they cannot touch you either.
After they leave, you search the drawers.
Feeling marine, feeling aquatic,
you find the ring you've never worn.

8.

So: you disdain what you desire.
I know the type.
Not even the ring you took from your son
who had it from your father can set you straight.
Slip it onto your finger. It will change nothing.

The Island: A Fable

Once upon a time there was an island,
green and lush, long as a shoestring,
with tall mountains and fertile valleys.

The inhabitants were a happy, if raucous,
people. They were ruled by a family
of kings, of great and marvelous power.

The kings held sway over all the island
and over many other islands also,
and even over part of the continent.

To protect the kingdom from invaders,
the people built moats everywhere,
sea moats with mud, land moats with water.

The royal palace was guarded by iron gates
and towers of stone hewn from the moats.
No one who entered was allowed to leave.

Inside the palace, where feasts were frequent,
fountains flowed with a wine airy and sweet,
tables were topped with treats for every taste.

So they lived for years longer than centuries,
secure in the knowledge that their island
was the most beautiful in the wide world.

One fine day the island sank into the ocean,
which rippled and bubbled softly welcoming
the kings and their people into its bosom.

Fatherly Thoughts on Mother's Day

Growing up has made
them someone else,
or worse, something else,

or worse still, their time's.
Here's my issue: possessives
drop away cruelly, careless

of the symmetries of love and need,
without regard for the former
fathers still fatherly, the ex-moms

still maternal, casualties all
of the apostrophe s. We keep
the house, the pool, the bank

accounts, but not our flesh.
Our flesh drifts away because
that's what we teach our flesh

to do. And we stay behind,
stripped and aching, orphans
of children no longer ours who,

as we say, are now on their own.

Piedra

He appeared at the door on Saturday mornings,
a crumpled paper bag in hand. A tall man,
his name was Piedra: long face, pocked cheeks,
combed-back gray hair. The boy's father would go
to the bedroom and emerge moments later with his wallet.
The bills changed hands and slipped into the bag.
Forty years later, the boy is on the phone with his son
thinking about Piedra, his pock marks, the brown paper bag.

The Last Exile

When he left his house he didn't turn off the TV,
not because he expected to come right back
but as a promise to himself that he would return.
Images of crowds hearing speeches lit up
the round screen for weeks, until the authorities
removed the furniture and padlocked the doors.
By then he was hundreds of miles away.

The years went by. He learned a new language.
Color televisions replaced black-and-white sets.
His children grew up, moved to places he never visited.
Forty years after leaving his country, he passed away,
survived by his wife, four children, seven grandchildren,
and a Zenith TV in a garbage heap somewhere in Havana.

Inside Andy Taylor

I'll tell you what it is about fishing.
It's not about the fish; it's about the water.
It must be I've an island inside me
because when I'm on that lake, no one around
but my boy, both of us surrounded by water,
it doesn't matter if we catch anything or not.

The man with the badge and the uniform
isn't me. The fisherman isn't me. The friend
and the boyfriend isn't me. The nephew isn't me.
The good neighbor and good guy isn't me.
Who I am is a man who loves to sit in a row boat
with his son, in the middle of a clear lake, doing nothing.
Like I said, there must be an island inside me.

Old Octopus

In the beginning he had many arms.
Now he bumps along the ocean's floor,
a lone tentacle slowly heaving,
sniffing out the madrepores.

"You say I vent to hide or threaten.
It's not so. Ink is connection.
I vent to embrace. I vent to hold you.
Armless, I yearn, I stay in motion.

My ink is thicker than your water, but
I am so small, a fist without fingers,
and you are everywhere. I do what I do.
I can't swim. I don't sleep. What I do is linger,

wait for the proper current. When it comes
—it is here, now—I flood the deep with longing."

After Exile

Cincuenta y cinco años más tarde, concluido el Diluvio, todos han abandonado el Arca—menos Noé.

Fifty-five years later, the Deluge long ended, everyone has left the Ark—except him.

II.

Dirty Old Man Watches the Birds

He has been doing this for fifteen years,
maybe more. He remembers putting up the birdfeeder,
how difficult it was to bury the metal pole
in the ground because, never having buried anything
except relatives, he didn't notice the corkscrew tip.
So he stabbed mightily at the red clay until the depth
of penetration immobilized the pole and its two hooks,
a little wooden cabin hanging from the taller one,
from the other a conical grill shaped like a shell casing.

A few days later, after the squirrels came,
he wrapped a black metal skirt around the pole to thwart them,
but skirts have never thwarted anybody. He hung a baffle instead.
Soon after he bought a pair of binoculars
and a book he still owns (because he still owns all the books
he's ever bought), *Birds of the Carolinas*.

Since then he's been watching the birds—his birds
—continuously, if one allows for intermittencies
such as travel, breakdowns in routine, and boredom.

When he started watching he wasn't old or dirty,
he was still young and eager, and it occurs to him
that he has changed more than his birds. A grackle,
top dog in his backyard birdland, always acts like a grackle,
throwing its weight and wings around as if it owned the joint.
A titmouse, with the pompadour that reminds him
of a 1950s teenager, will come to the birdfeeder only
if no one else is there. The nuthatch is a smaller
but more courageous titmouse. The regal cardinal behaves
regally, taking time to select the seeds most to its liking.
And then there are the finches, the only birds with a sense
of community. On a good summer day, half a dozen will perch
on the grill and peck, undisturbed and undisturbing.

Men like him are not so predictable. In his youth D.O.M.
swooped and squawked like a grackle; in middle age,
he regarded himself as a cardinal to-be (though others,
who knew him, thought him a grackle has-been).
Today, if he had companionable wings, he'd be a finch
in the midst of finches. But life being what it shouldn't be,
he is one nuthatch away from turning into a titmouse.

Dirty Old Man Looks for Same

When he was growing up, people like him
were everywhere. His father was a D.O.M.,
as were his uncles and great uncles.
But that was another time and place.
Now D.O.M. are as rare as white deer.

If there were a club of D.O.M., he thinks,
as there are garden and book and country clubs,
his life would be improved.
The club would be called DOMUS.
In between trips to the bathroom,
he and his kind would sip something alcoholic,
smoke cigarettes, trade stories, fictional and maybe not.

Every once in a while, he would have something to tell,
like the time he flirted with the beautiful dermatologist
and she wrote her number on the back of the prescription
for rosacea. But she must have retired by now,
he realizes, and off somewhere in the Outer Banks
painting beach landscapes.

After years of trying within and without
his family to recruit for the club, he has concluded
that Dirty Old Men are a dying breed.

From the web: "Suffice it to say, if you ever
see a white deer, you are one of the lucky few."

Dirty Old Man Regrets

For eight or ten years he has asked himself
why sleeping with her ruined the friendship;
why making love, or rather, having intercourse
once only should break a bond of many years
and endless conversations in two languages,
the way a sudden shower spoils a silk suit
if you don't have an umbrella. Had he thought
about it, he would have thought that intimacy
of long-standing was the umbrella over them,
even in the double bed of a motel in Buffalo.
But when she said, after he was through,
ok, get off now, he should have realized that,
somewhere, he had forgotten his umbrella.

Dirty Old Man Applies for Medicare

It was all going well, smooth as silt
(he knows it's silk but he likes silt better),
until the virtual genie needed to know
the date when he became an American.
He remembered the decade, diabolic
nineteen seventies, but nothing else.

In this predicament, what do you do?
If you're like him, you call your ex-wife,
at whose behest, naturally, he naturalized.
It was she who found the witnesses,
the Jewish couple from across the street,
who swore to his good moral character

because they knew her. Since he and she
divorced twenty-five years ago, she is
still sore. So she tells him that she has
nothing that belongs to him. Pressed,
she tells him that his citizening occured
before they knew each other, to which

he replies that they never knew each other.
After she hangs up, he gets back at his ex
by screaming at his not-ex for hours.
The next morning, as he's about to shovel snow,
the ex calls. Not admitting error (the only
error she will admit to is having married him),

she says that she found the form. Will leave
it in an envelope by her door. No need to knock.

Dirty Old Man Feeling Bereft

He loves them (chastely, he's not that dirty)
and they leave him. Every four months they
leave him. For forty years they have been leaving

him and still he can't resign himself. He sees
them cap their pens, gather up their notebooks
(now their tablets and laptops), for the last time.

Then he watches them walk out the door
with a smile and a wave, or sometimes with nothing.
At least they're not my children, he thinks.

They don't know it, but he needs them more
than they need him. Classes interrupt
their lives. For him, teaching them is his life.

Today he repeated the same line he always uses:
This class, he said, is a marriage with an expiration date.
It worked. He wants them to feel abandoned too.

Now he will spend weeks remembering all the things
he forgot to say to them, that quotation from Joyce,
the bilingual joke about nuns, the sexy story of his dissertation.

Dirty Old Man Takes a Nap

He dreams of strawberries—wild, exorbitant
strawberries, potato-shaped, poisonous and not.

Carriers of a disease he calls Night Shadow,
the toxic fruit grows beyond the railroad ties
that he laid down for his wife's vegetable garden.
If you bite into one, it kills you on the spot.
The others, inside the square of ties, also look
grotesque but they are harmless—and delicious.

As he naps, he frets about the grandchildren
he doesn't have not knowing which are which.
He walks around gazing at the ripe red lumps
and marveling at nature's treachery. To think
that someone he loves could be slain by a strawberry.

After he wakes up, he recounts the dream
to Mrs. D.O.M., as is his custom. She says to him:
My dear, dear Dirty Old Man, you never change.
Familiar things in unfamiliar places always scare you.

Dirty Old Man Loses His Place

When the alarm goes off in the middle of the night, he jumps out of bed and goes looking for a chair. Problem is, he doesn't know where he is. For other people, two homes are a sign of status; for D.O.M. it's one more reason to be confused. In the dark, he rushes around inside the house that's not there looking for a dining room that's somewhere else to reset a smoke alarm that doesn't exist.

As he turns a corner that does not lead to the kitchen, he crashes into Mrs. D.O.M. Normally mild and gentle, she pushes him out of the way. When she finally turns off the alarm, D.O.M. is still searching for a chair to stand on. She grabs him by the sleeve of his silk pajamas. It's the door, she says. D.O.M. stares at her. It's the front door. You must have left it open.

D.O.M. is sure that he closed and locked every door, as he does every night no matter which house he thinks he's in. He would like to say to his wife: It wasn't me, *cariño*, it was the house ghosts. They didn't want to trip the smoke alarm, and so they went outside to light their cigars. But he can tell that Mrs. D.O.M., who has had a long life and an even longer night, is in no mood for old-country ghost stories. He shuffles back to the bedroom with the air of a man who can't explain himself.

Dirty Old Man Foams at the Mouth

Yes, it doesn't take much, Mrs. D.O.M. confirms in an interview. Another time we were in the car listening to the Sinatra channel on the radio when my husband blurts out, He should be shot! Who? I say, knowing that his list of candidates for execution is almost endless. He names the legendary singer who at that very moment was in the act of committing the crime of singing "I'll Be Seeing You," Johnny Carson's favorite song and thus a favorite also with D.O.M., backed by a big orchestra and an up-tempo, nelson-riddleish arrangement. D.O.M. then spends the rest of the trip—with him, a short jaunt to the gym can turn into a journey of a thousand miles—explaining why anyone with half an ounce of brains and even a smidgen of artistic sense would not do such a thing to a lovely song. We're already in the parking lot, it's fifteen degrees outside and I'm freezing, and he's still fulminating about aesthetic fitness, the sanctity of the Great American Songbook, and only the D.O.M. God knows what else. It's too bad they didn't consult you, dear, I say, as we finally make it into the gym, where D.O.M. spends the next hour thinking up additional arguments why the swinging version of "I'll Be Seeing You" should be banned from the universe. I don't have to tell you what the trip back from the gym was like.

Dirty Old Man Thinks about the Future

He wonders how will they remember him, the granddaughters
bequeathed by marriage. Sullen or silly,
curtained in smoke or lunging for the *chorizo*,
the man who mumbled in a strange tongue
and couldn't make himself understood even in English.

He hardly ever spoke to us, they'll say,
kissed us vaguely in the vicinity of our heads
and often missed. Some evenings through
the living room window we'd see them dancing,
Tavo and Gram, which we thought was funny.

What I remember, Mary Emma will say to Charlotte,
is the time I grabbed a cigar from his hand
and his eyes blazed. Tavo was different, Charlotte will say.
He was there for many years, always with Gram,
and then he wasn't and it was as if he had never been.

Dirty Old Man Eschews a Fling

D.O.M. was happy to play along,
ride her smile, tamp her temper,
until she proposed a midday tryst.

When he refused, she threatened
to dig her high heels into his eye sockets
(only a metaphor, she explained).

The next day she parks herself
outside his house. Reluctant
to stake his life on a figure of speech,

he stays inside, peering through the shades.
In the old days D.O.M. paid the price.
If he made love to a woman, he slept with her.

Now, well into his seventh decade,
he still searches the coverts,
hoping to spot a fox mad enough

to run with him, young enough
to be worth the chase, and wise enough
not to wish to get caught.

Dirty Old Man Talks to Himself in the Dark

I've had great uncles, he says.
I've had great uncles and great great-uncles.
Tío Pepe taught me how to be what I am.
The last time I saw him he was in the Catholic hospital
flirting with the nurse, moments before he lapsed into a coma.
Tío Mike taught me that a dirty old man
is not necessarily a dirty old man.
The last time I saw him he was mixing a martini.
Tío Pedro taught me to be strong beyond madness.
The last time I saw him I didn't really see him.
He was sitting in a lawn chair in the yard
in the middle of the night. All I could see
was the glowing tip of his cigar, a firefly.
I never saw him, them, again—in the flesh,
because I'm seeing them now, just as they were
the last time, not the last time, I saw them.

Dirty Old Man Talks to His Neighbors

Contemplating retirement,
D.O.M. asks his neighbors,
all retired, how they spend
their time. I garden, says one.
D.O.M. thinks: Gardening
is not a manly occupation.
I make furniture, says another.
D.O.M. thinks: I've never made
anything in my life, nor ever will.
He asks a third, who replies:
I twist in the wind, when there is one.
And what if there is no wind, neighbor?
I twist and make my own.
Finally, D.O.M. thinks,
a man after my own heart.

Dirty Old Man Argues with His Wife

For fifteen years he and his wife have been arguing
about a song. She says it's a song about young love
gone wrong. He says it's a bitter, hit-bottom lament
by a middle-aged man (like he used to be)

whose much younger paramour has jilted him.
She says that only a young girl (like she used to be)
could say, credibly, that she forgot to eat and sleep
and pray because of how much she was in love.

He says the speaker is exaggerating, as when he compares
himself to a child of three. She says the only reason
for the number is the rhyme. He replies that it doesn't make
sense for Sinatra to sound like love-sick teenager

when he was trying to get over Ava. His wife comes back
with a shut-him-up riposte: He sang "My Way," didn't he?
And so they go on, happily eristic, a song of innocence
or of experience, depending on who doesn't want to argue.

Dirty Old Man Endeavors to Be Optimistic

He has been inside
himself all day,
but for an occasional glance at the snow.

A roomy clutter
in there, where
he is, trap doors to avoid, unexpected

vistas as comp-
ensation. The dead
days between Christmas and New Year's

Eve get the worst
of him. He wonders
why sorrow, such a lovely word, has fallen

from fashion.
He can't take
a pill for sorrow. There is no medication

for yearn, the
other lovely word
he finds inside, tucked away in a drawer,

a loose leaf
from a binder
or a bush where cardinals perched last year.

A writer and scholar, Cuban-born **Gustavo Pérez Firmat** is the author of several books, among them *Life on the Hyphen*, a study of Cuban American culture that was awarded the Eugene M. Kayden University Press National Book Award, and the memoir *Next Year in Cuba*, which was nominated for a Pulitzer Prize. His poems and stories have appeared in many anthologies, including *The Oxford Book of Caribbean Verse, Growing Up in the South, The Prentice Hall Anthology of Latino Literature, Cubanísimo: The Vintage Book of Contemporary Cuban Literature*. His most recent books are *The Havana Habit* and *A Cuban in Mayberry*. He is a fellow of the American Academy of Arts and Sciences and has been the recipient of fellowships from the National Endowment for the Humanities, the American Council of Learned Societies, and the John Simon Guggenheim Memorial Foundation. *Newsweek* included him among "100 Americans to watch for the 21st century" and *Hispanic Business Magazine* selected him as one of the "100 most influential Hispanics" in the United States. He teaches Spanish American literature at Columbia University, where he is the David Feinson Professor in the Humanities.

www.ingramcontent.com/pod-product-compliance
Lightning Source LLC
Chambersburg PA
CBHW060225050426
42446CB00013B/3171